Basics of Meteorology

Weather measurements instruments

Weather patterns and systems

Factors influencing climate

Weather forecasting

Weather hazards and safety

Weather and society

Weather phenomenon

Historical weather events

Future Trends in Meteorology

Basics of Meteorology

Meteorology

Meteorology is the study of the Earth's atmosphere and the weather that happens in it. Think of the atmosphere like a big blanket of air that surrounds our planet. It's made up of different gases like nitrogen, oxygen, and tiny particles.

The atmosphere is divided into layers, and the one we live in is called the troposphere. This layer is where all the action happens, like clouds, rain, and storms.

Weather

Weather is what happens in the atmosphere at a particular place and time. It includes things like temperature, humidity (how much moisture is in the air), wind speed and direction, and air pressure.

Temperature

Temperature tells us how hot or cold the air is. It's measured using a thermometer.

Humidity is how humid or muggy it feels outside. Wind speed tells us how fast the air is moving, and wind direction tells us which way it's blowing.

Air pressure is the weight of the air pushing down on us. High pressure usually means fair weather, while low pressure can bring clouds and rain.

Weather measurements instruments

Thermometer:

Measures temperature. It consists of a glass tube with a bulb at one end filled with a liquid like mercury or alcohol. As the temperature changes, the liquid expands or contracts, and the reading on the scale indicates the temperature.

Barometer

Measures air pressure. There are two main types: mercury barometers and aneroid barometers.

Mercury barometers use a column of mercury to measure air pressure, while aneroid barometers use a flexible metal box that expands or contracts with changes in air pressure.

Hygrometer:

Measures humidity or moisture content in the air. There are various types of hygrometers, including psychrometers (which use wet and dry bulb thermometers) and electronic hygrometers (which use sensors to measure humidity).

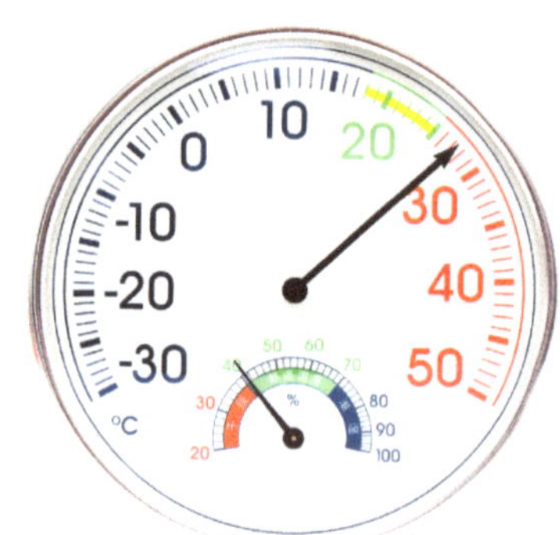

Anemometer:

Measures wind speed and direction. Anemometers come in different designs, but most consist of cups that catch the wind and rotate, generating a signal that can be used to determine wind speed. Some anemometers also have a vane or windsock to indicate wind direction.

Rain Gauge:

Measures the amount of precipitation (rain, snow, sleet) that falls over a specific period.

It typically consists of a cylinder with a funnel-shaped top to collect precipitation, and a measuring tube to measure the accumulated water

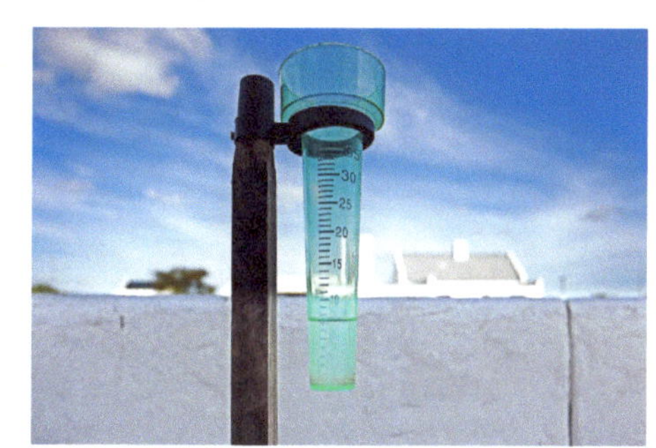

Weather Balloon:

Carries instruments such as radiosondes into the atmosphere to collect data on temperature, humidity, air pressure, and wind speed at different altitudes. The data collected helps meteorologists make weather forecasts.

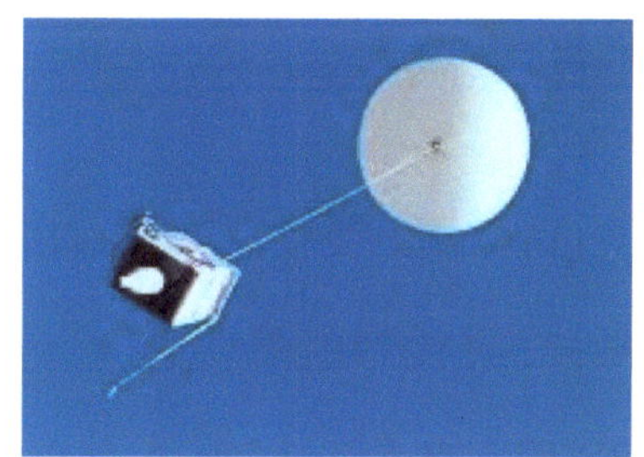

Weather Station:

A collection of instruments, including those mentioned above, that continuously measure and record various weather parameters like temperature, humidity, pressure, wind speed, and precipitation. Weather stations can be automated or operated manually.

Weather patterns and systems

Weather patterns and systems refer to the recurring atmospheric conditions and phenomena that influence weather over specific regions and time periods. Here are some common weather patterns and systems:

High-pressure systems:

Areas where air sinks and spreads out, leading to clear skies, light winds, and generally fair weather. High-pressure systems are associated with stable atmospheric conditions.

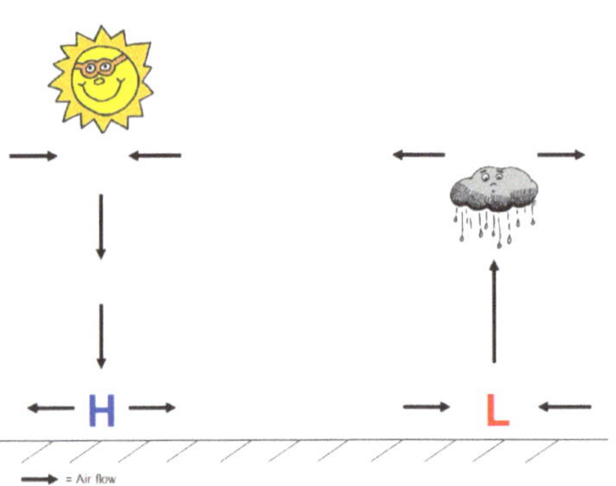

Low-pressure systems:

Areas where air rises and converges, creating clouds, precipitation, and often unsettled weather.

Low-pressure systems are associated with cyclonic circulation and can bring rain, storms, and strong winds.

Fronts:

Boundaries between air masses with different temperatures and moisture levels. There are several types of fronts, including:

Cold front: Forms when a cold air mass advances and displaces a warmer air mass, leading to potentially severe weather, such as thunderstorms and heavy rain.

Warm front: Forms when a warm air mass advances and rises over a cold air mass, resulting in gradual cloudiness, light precipitation, and warmer temperatures.

Stationary front: Occurs when neither air mass displaces the other, resulting in prolonged periods of cloudy weather and light precipitation.

Occluded front: Forms when a fast-moving cold front overtakes a slower-moving warm front, resulting in complex weather patterns, including precipitation and temperature changes.

Tropical cyclones:

Large-scale, low-pressure systems that form over warm ocean waters and can develop into hurricanes, typhoons, or cyclones, depending on their location. These intense storms are characterized by strong winds, heavy rain, and storm surges.

Thunderstorms

Atmospheric disturbances characterized by the presence of thunder, lightning, heavy rain, and sometimes hail or tornadoes. Thunderstorms form when warm, moist air rises rapidly, leading to the development of cumulonimbus clouds.

El Niño and La Niña:

Climate phenomena associated with periodic changes in sea surface temperatures in the equatorial Pacific Ocean. El Niño events typically bring warmer-than-average sea surface temperatures and can lead to weather disruptions worldwide, while La Niña events bring cooler-than-average sea surface temperatures and can also influence global weather patterns.

Climate and climate change

Climate refers to the long-term patterns of temperature, precipitation, humidity, wind, and other atmospheric conditions in a particular region or across the globe.

It represents the average weather conditions over a period of at least 30 years, providing insight into the typical atmospheric behavior of an area.

Factors influencing climate include

Latitude

Distance from the equator affects the amount of sunlight received, influencing temperature patterns.

Altitude

Elevation above sea level affects temperature and precipitation patterns, with higher altitudes generally experiencing cooler temperatures.

Proximity to water bodies:

Coastal areas often have milder climates due to the moderating effect of oceans, while continental interiors experience more extreme temperature variations.

Ocean currents: Ocean currents transport heat and moisture, influencing climate patterns along coastal regions.

Atmospheric circulation:

Global wind patterns and pressure systems play a role in redistributing heat and moisture around the planet, shaping climate zones.

Greenhouse gas emissions

Human activities, including burning fossil fuels, deforestation, and industrial processes, release greenhouse gases (e.g., carbon dioxide, methane) into the atmosphere, enhancing the natural greenhouse effect and leading to global warming.

Deforestation

Clearing forests for agriculture, urbanization, and other purposes reduces the Earth's capacity to absorb carbon dioxide, contributing to increased atmospheric concentrations of greenhouse gases.

Land use changes:

Alterations in land use, such as urbanization and agricultural expansion, can impact local and regional climate patterns through changes in surface albedo, evapotranspiration, and land surface temperatures.

Industrial processes:

Industrial activities release pollutants and aerosols into the atmosphere, which can affect cloud formation, precipitation patterns, and regional climate variability.

Natural factors:

Natural variations in solar radiation, volcanic eruptions, and ocean-atmosphere interactions also influence climate variability, although human-induced factors currently dominate the observed trends in global climate change.

The consequences of climate change include

1. Rising global temperatures
2. Changes in precipitation patterns, leading to droughts or floods
3. Sea level rise due to melting ice caps and thermal expansion of seawater
4. Shifts in ecosystems and biodiversity
5. Impacts on agriculture, water resources, human health, and economies

6. Addressing climate change requires international cooperation, mitigation efforts to reduce greenhouse gas emissions, adaptation strategies to cope with the impacts of climate change, and investments in renewable energy, sustainable land management, and conservation initiatives.

Weather forecasting

Weather forecasting is the process of predicting future atmospheric conditions based on observations of current weather patterns and using various scientific methods and tools. Here's an overview of how weather forecasting works

Data collection: Meteorologists collect data from various sources, including weather stations, satellites, radar systems, weather balloons, ocean buoys, and aircraft. These observations provide information on temperature, humidity, air pressure, wind speed and direction, cloud cover, and precipitation.

Data analysis:

Meteorologists analyze the collected data to identify patterns, trends, and atmospheric conditions that influence weather.

They use computer models and numerical weather prediction techniques to simulate the behavior of the atmosphere and make forecasts.

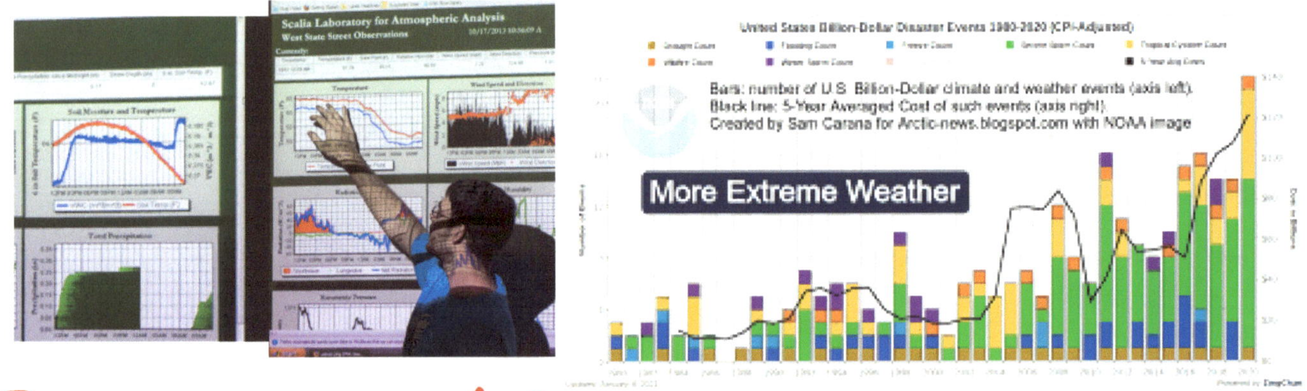

Forecast models:

Weather forecast models are mathematical representations of the atmosphere that simulate the interactions between different atmospheric variables over time.

These models divide the atmosphere into a grid of points and use equations to calculate changes in temperature, pressure, wind, and other variables at each point over time.

Initialization: Forecast models are initialized using current weather observations to provide an initial state of the atmosphere. This initialization process helps the model simulate the current weather conditions accurately and improves the accuracy of the forecast.

Prediction: Once initialized, weather forecast models simulate the future evolution of the atmosphere over a specific time period, typically ranging from a few hours to several days or even weeks.

Meteorologists analyze the model output to generate weather forecasts for different regions, including temperature forecasts, precipitation forecasts, wind forecasts, and severe weather outlooks.

Interpretation and communication

Meteorologists interpret the forecast model output and communicate the forecast to the public through various channels, including television, radio, websites, mobile apps, and social media.

They provide information on expected weather conditions, potential hazards, and recommended actions to stay safe.

Weather forecasting is a complex and continually evolving field that relies on advances in technology, scientific research, and observational capabilities to provide accurate and timely weather information to the public and decision-makers.

Weather hazards and safety

Weather hazards refer to dangerous or potentially damaging weather conditions that pose risks to people, property, and the environment. It's crucial to understand these hazards and take appropriate safety measures to protect yourself and others. Here are some common weather hazards and safety tips:

Thunderstorms:

Hazard: Thunderstorms can produce lightning, heavy rain, strong winds, hail, and tornadoes, leading to property damage, injuries, and fatalities.

Safety tips:

When thunder roars, go indoors! Seek shelter in a sturdy building or a car with a hardtop.

Avoid open fields, high ground, isolated trees, and bodies of water during thunderstorms.

Stay away from metal objects, water, and electronic devices that can conduct electricity.

If caught outdoors with no shelter, crouch low to the ground, but avoid lying flat.

Tornadoes:

Hazard: Tornadoes are violently rotating columns of air that can cause extensive damage to buildings and infrastructure, as well as injuries and fatalities.

Safety tips:

Have a tornado safety plan in place and designate a safe room or shelter area in your home, preferably in a basement or interior room on the lowest floor.

If a tornado warning is issued, seek shelter immediately in a sturdy building or underground shelter.

Stay away from windows, doors, and exterior walls during a tornado.

If you are caught outdoors or in a vehicle, seek shelter in a low-lying area, such as a ditch, and cover your head.

Hurricanes:

Hazard: Hurricanes are powerful tropical storms with high winds, heavy rain, storm surges, and flooding that can cause widespread destruction and loss of life.

Safety tips:

Follow evacuation orders issued by local authorities if you live in a hurricane-prone area.

Prepare an emergency kit with essential supplies, including food, water, medications, flashlight, batteries, and important documents.

Board up windows and secure outdoor objects to prevent damage from flying debris.

Stay indoors during the storm and away from windows and exterior doors.

Flooding:

Hazard: Flooding occurs when water overflows onto land that is normally dry, leading to property damage, road closures, and the risk of drowning.

Safety tips:

Avoid driving or walking through flooded areas, as just six inches of moving water can knock you down, and two feet of water can sweep away most vehicles.

Move to higher ground if you are in a flood-prone area and follow evacuation orders if instructed.

Keep important documents and valuables in a waterproof container and elevate utilities in your home to minimize flood damage.

Winter storms:

Hazard:

Winter storms can bring snow, ice, freezing rain, and cold temperatures, leading to hazardous driving conditions, power outages, and hypothermia.

Safety tips:

Stay indoors during a winter storm and avoid unnecessary travel.

Dress warmly in layers and limit time spent outdoors in extreme cold.

Use caution when walking or driving on icy surfaces and allow extra time for braking.

Keep emergency supplies in your home and vehicle, including blankets, food, water, and a flashlight.

Weather and society

Weather has significant impacts on various aspects of society, influencing human activities, economies, and public health. Here's how weather interacts with society:

Agriculture:

Weather conditions, such as temperature, precipitation, and sunlight, play a crucial role in crop growth, livestock health, and agricultural productivity.

Farmers rely on weather forecasts to make decisions about planting, irrigation, fertilization, and harvesting.

Extreme weather events, such as droughts, floods, and heatwaves, can devastate crops, leading to food shortages and economic losses.

Transportation:

Weather affects transportation systems, including road, air, and maritime travel.

Severe weather conditions, such as snowstorms, heavy rain, fog, and high winds, can disrupt traffic, cause accidents, and lead to flight delays and cancellations.

Transportation agencies use weather forecasts to monitor road conditions, adjust schedules, and implement safety measures to protect travelers and minimize disruptions.

Energy:

Weather influences energy demand and supply patterns, particularly in sectors such as heating, cooling, and electricity generation.

Hot weather increases the demand for air conditioning, while cold weather drives up heating requirements. Weather-sensitive industries, such as agriculture, manufacturing, and construction, also rely on energy resources affected by weather conditions.

Renewable energy sources, such as solar and wind power, are dependent on weather patterns for their generation capacity.

Health

Weather impacts human health and well-being, affecting factors such as heat-related illnesses, respiratory conditions, and infectious diseases.

Extreme temperatures, heatwaves, and poor air quality can exacerbate health problems, particularly among vulnerable populations such as the elderly, children, and individuals with pre-existing medical conditions.

Weather forecasts help public health officials implement heat advisories, air quality alerts, and other measures to protect public health during extreme weather events.

Emergency management

Weather-related disasters, such as hurricanes, tornadoes, floods, wildfires, and earthquakes, pose significant challenges for emergency management agencies and first responders.

Weather forecasts and early warning systems are essential for monitoring potential hazards, issuing evacuation orders, coordinating response efforts, and providing assistance to affected communities.

Public education and preparedness initiatives help individuals and communities mitigate risks and improve resilience to weather-related disasters.

Overall, weather has wide-ranging impacts on society, shaping daily activities, economic outcomes, public health, and emergency preparedness.

By understanding the relationship between weather and society, stakeholders can better anticipate and respond to weather-related challenges and opportunities.

Weather phenomenon

Weather phenomena are natural occurrences in the atmosphere that can be observed and studied. These phenomena often result from the interactions of various atmospheric factors such as temperature, humidity, air pressure, and wind. Here are some common weather phenomena:

Clouds: Clouds are visible masses of water droplets or ice crystals suspended in the atmosphere. They come in various shapes and sizes, including cumulus (puffy and white), stratus (layered and gray), and cirrus (thin and wispy). Clouds play a crucial role in the Earth's energy balance and weather patterns.

Precipitation: Precipitation refers to any form of water, liquid or solid, that falls from the atmosphere to the Earth's surface. Common types of precipitation include rain, snow, sleet, and hail. Precipitation is a vital component of the Earth's water cycle and influences weather, climate, and ecosystems.

Thunderstorms:

Thunderstorms are atmospheric disturbances characterized by the presence of thunder, lightning, heavy rain, and sometimes hail or tornadoes.

They form when warm, moist air rises rapidly, leading to the development of cumulonimbus clouds and vertical motion in the atmosphere.

Lightning

Lightning is a sudden and powerful electrical discharge that occurs within thunderstorms.

It results from the buildup and release of electrical charges within clouds and between clouds and the ground. Lightning poses risks to people, property, and the environment and can cause wildfires, power outages, and injuries or fatalities.

Tornadoes:

Tornadoes are violently rotating columns of air that extend from thunderstorms to the ground. They are one of the most destructive weather phenomena, capable of causing widespread damage and loss of life. Tornadoes typically form within severe thunderstorms and are associated with strong winds, flying debris, and intense atmospheric pressure gradients.

Hurricanes

Hurricanes, also known as tropical cyclones or typhoons, are powerful tropical storms with sustained winds of at least 74 miles per hour (119 kilometers per hour). They form over warm ocean waters and can cause extensive damage to coastal areas through high winds, storm surges, heavy rain, and flooding.

Fog: Fog is a type of low-lying cloud that forms near the Earth's surface when air cools and becomes saturated with moisture, causing water droplets to condense. Fog reduces visibility and can create hazardous driving conditions, particularly in areas with dense fog.

Rainbow: A rainbow is a meteorological phenomenon caused by the refraction, dispersion, and reflection of sunlight in water droplets in the atmosphere. Rainbows appear as arcs of color in the sky, typically following a rain shower or during other instances of sunlight and rain.

These weather phenomena are just a few examples of the diverse and fascinating processes that occur in the Earth's atmosphere. Studying and understanding these phenomena helps meteorologists forecast weather, scientists understand climate patterns, and individuals appreciate the beauty and power of nature.

Historical weather events

Historical weather events are significant weather occurrences that have left a mark on society, either through their impact on human lives, infrastructure, or the environment. Here are some examples of notable historical weather events:

The Great Galveston Hurricane (1900):

This devastating hurricane struck Galveston, Texas, on September 8, 1900, causing widespread destruction and an estimated 6,000 to 12,000 fatalities, making it the deadliest natural disaster in U.S. history.

The Dust Bowl (1930s)

A severe drought and dust storms affected large parts of the Great Plains in the United States during the 1930s. The Dust Bowl caused extensive crop failures, soil erosion, and economic hardship for farmers, leading to significant migration and changes in agricultural practices.

The Heat Wave of 2003 (Europe)

A prolonged heatwave struck Europe in the summer of 2003, resulting in record-breaking temperatures and thousands of heat-related deaths across the continent.

The heatwave highlighted the vulnerability of populations to extreme heat events and raised concerns about the impacts of climate change on heatwaves.

Hurricane Katrina (2005):

Hurricane Katrina made landfall in Louisiana on August 29, 2005, causing catastrophic flooding in New Orleans and along the Gulf Coast. The storm resulted in more than 1,800 fatalities and billions of dollars in damage, making it one of the costliest and deadliest hurricanes in U.S. history.

The Tohoku Earthquake and Tsunami (2011):

A powerful magnitude 9.0 earthquake struck off the coast of Japan on March 11, 2011, triggering a massive tsunami that inundated coastal areas and caused widespread destruction and loss of life.

The disaster resulted in nearly 16,000 deaths, as well as damage to nuclear power plants and long-term environmental impacts.

The California Drought (2012-2016)

California experienced one of its most severe droughts on record from 2012 to 2016, leading to water shortages, crop failures, wildfires, and environmental degradation.

The drought highlighted the vulnerability of water resources in the face of climate variability and increased demand.

Superstorm Sandy (2012):

Superstorm Sandy, also known as Hurricane Sandy, struck the northeastern United States in October 2012, causing extensive flooding, power outages, and damage to coastal communities from storm surge and high winds. The storm resulted in dozens of fatalities and billions of dollars in damage.

These historical weather events serve as reminders of the power and unpredictability of nature and the importance of preparedness, resilience, and adaptation in the face of extreme weather and climate events.

Studying these events helps scientists, policymakers, and communities better understand and respond to future challenges related to weather and climate variability

Future Trends in Meteorology

As meteorology continues to evolve, several trends are shaping the field's future direction. Here are some key trends in meteorology:

Advances in technology: Continued advancements in technology, such as high-performance computing, remote sensing, and data analytics, are revolutionizing meteorological research, observation, and forecasting capabilities.

These technological innovations enable more accurate and timely weather predictions, as well as improved understanding of atmospheric processes and climate dynamics.

Integration of big data and artificial intelligence:

Meteorologists are increasingly leveraging big data analytics and artificial intelligence (AI) techniques, such as machine learning and neural networks, to analyze vast amounts of observational and model data, identify patterns, and improve weather forecasting accuracy.

AI-based algorithms can enhance the interpretation of complex atmospheric phenomena and provide valuable insights for forecasters and researchers.

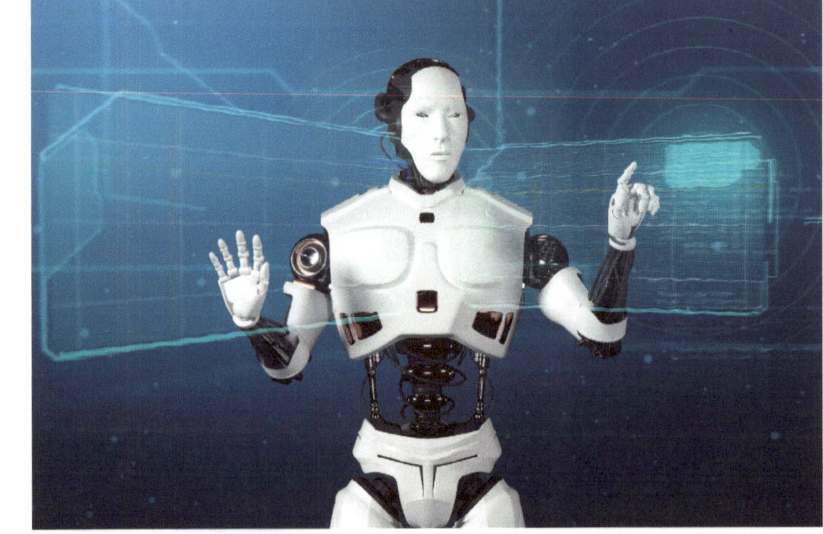

Advances in numerical weather prediction (NWP) models are enabling meteorologists to simulate atmospheric processes at increasingly higher resolutions, capturing finer-scale features and improving the accuracy of weather forecasts. High-resolution models enhance the prediction of localized weather phenomena, such as thunderstorms, hurricanes, and heavy precipitation events, and provide more detailed guidance for decision-making.

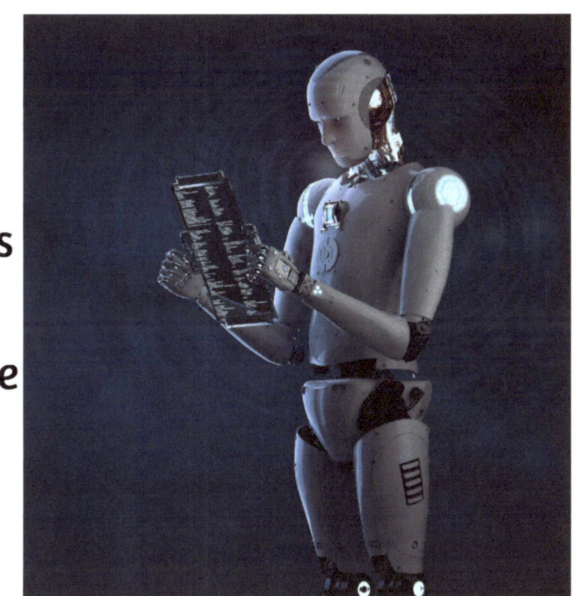

Earth system modeling: Meteorologists are expanding their focus beyond weather forecasting to include the study of Earth's interconnected systems, including the atmosphere, oceans, land surface, and cryosphere. Earth system models integrate multiple components of the Earth's climate system and enable researchers to investigate complex interactions and feedbacks, improve climate projections, and assess the impacts of human activities on global climate change.

Climate services and adaptation: There is growing recognition of the need for climate services that provide tailored information, tools, and resources to support decision-making and adaptation efforts in response to climate variability and change. Meteorologists play a key role in providing climate information and forecasts to help governments, businesses, and communities prepare for and mitigate the impacts of climate-related hazards, such as extreme weather events, sea-level rise, and changing precipitation patterns.

1.The process by which water changes from a liquid to a gas is called
____________.

2.The boundary between two air masses with different temperatures
and humidity levels is called a ____________.

3.Lightning is a discharge of ____________
between charged regions in the atmosphere.

4.The area of low atmospheric pressure at the center of a tropical
cyclone is called the ____________.

5.A severe localized storm characterized by strong winds, heavy
rain, lightning, and thunder is called a ____________.

6.The average weather conditions of a region over a long period,
typically 30 years, is known as ____________.

7.The process of predicting future weather conditions based on
current observations and scientific methods is called ____________.

8.A rotating column of air extending from a thunderstorm to the
ground is known as a ____________.

9.The phenomenon caused by the interaction of sunlight with
water droplets in the atmosphere, resulting in a spectrum of light,
is called a ____________.

10.The atmospheric layer closest to the Earth's surface, where
weather occurs, is called the ____________.

1. Evaporation
2. Front
3. Electricity
4. Eye
5. Thunderstorm
6. Climate
7. Weather forecasting
8. Tornado
9. Rainbow
10. Troposphere

www.ingramcontent.com/pod-product-compliance
Lightning Source LLC
Chambersburg PA
CBHW040207240726
48664CB00002B/865